MODERN ROLE MODELS

Tim Duncan

Chuck Bednar

Mason Crest Publishers

Produced by OTTN Publishing in association with
21st Century Publishing and Communications, Inc.

MASON CREST PUBLISHERS INC.
370 Reed Road
Broomall, Pennsylvania 19008
(866) MCP-BOOK (toll free)
www.masoncrest.com

Printed in the United States of America.

First Printing

9 8 7 6 5 4 3 2 1

Library of Congress Cataloging-in-Publication Data

Bednar, Chuck, 1976–
    Tim Duncan / Chuck Bednar.
        p. cm. — (Modern role models)
    Includes bibliographical references.
    ISBN-13: 978-1-4222-0481-8 (hardcover) — ISBN-13: 978-1-4222-0768-0 (pbk.)
    ISBN-10: 1-4222-0481-2 (hardcover)
    1. Duncan, Tim, 1976–   —Juvenile literature. 2. Basketball players—United
States—Biography. I. Title.
GV884.D86B43 2009
796.323092—dc22
[B]   2008020406

Publisher's note:
All quotations in this book come from original sources, and contain the spelling and grammatical inconsistencies of the original text.

CROSS-CURRENTS

In the ebb and flow of the currents of life we are each influenced by many people, places, and events that we directly experience or have learned about. Throughout the chapters of this book you will come across **CROSS-CURRENTS** *reference boxes. These boxes direct you to a* **CROSS-CURRENTS** *section in the back of the book that contains fascinating and informative sidebars and related pictures. Go on.* ▸▸

CONTENTS

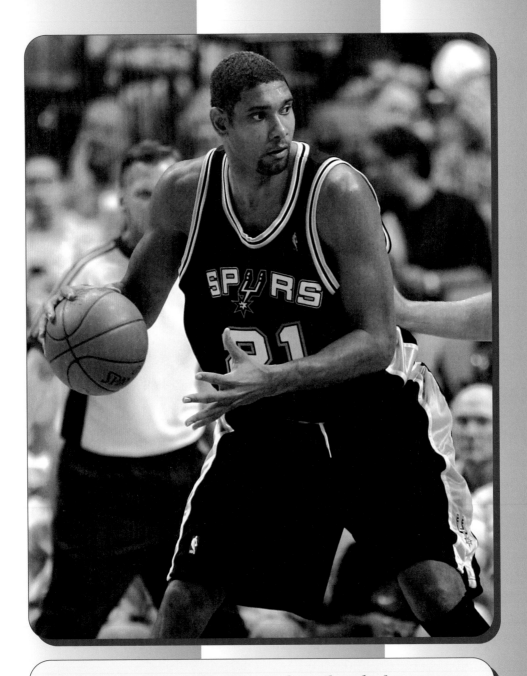

San Antonio Spurs' Tim Duncan in action during a game against the Dallas Mavericks, October 9, 2007. The San Antonio center is one of the best players in NBA history. Since entering the league in the 1997–98 season, Tim has led the Spurs to four NBA championships. His San Antonio teams won titles in 1999, 2003, 2005, and 2007.

1

A True Champion

THE ROAD TO THE NATIONAL BASKETBALL ASSO-ciation (NBA) Finals can be long and difficult. For Tim Duncan, however, that path has become very familiar. In 2007, when Duncan led his San Antonio Spurs to the professional basketball championship series, it was the fourth time he had headed down that road.

In the 2007 finals, LeBron James and the Cleveland Cavaliers would provide the opposition for Duncan and the Spurs. While San Antonio had overcome the Denver Nuggets, Phoenix Suns, and Utah Jazz to win the Western Conference, the Cavs had defeated the Washington Wizards, New Jersey Nets, and Detroit Pistons in the East. The Spurs were undefeated in their three previous NBA Finals appearances, but Cleveland had beaten them in the two games the teams played during the 2006–07 season. With that history, the two teams locked horns starting on June 7. Tim intended once

CROSS-CURRENTS

If you'd like to learn more about the early history of Tim's team, read "The San Antonio Spurs." Go to page 48.

again to lead his teammates to the promised land and bring home NBA title number four.

PERCEPTION VS. REALITY

Many people believed that LeBron James would be the NBA's next big star, the guy who would forge a legacy greater than Michael Jordan's. He was the future of the league, the high school phenom that fans and the media called King James in anticipation of a great career. While LeBron was an excellent player, it would be hard for anyone to live up to the massive hype surrounding him. His face was plastered all over television, in commercial after commercial promoting product after product. He even had his own comic book.

Tim Duncan was just the opposite. He was a low-key, blue-collar star. He played fundamentally solid basketball and got the job done, and his teammates followed suit. Still, the buzz was that Tim was not exciting to watch, even if he was one of the top players in the league and a two-time **MVP**—and especially not when compared to the much flashier James. The 2007 Finals was shaping up to be a clash between perception and reality; a battle between the man who would be king and the one who had quietly worn the crown throughout much of his career.

CROSS-CURRENTS

To find out about another dominant basketball center whose career preceded Tim Duncan's, check out "Bill Russell." Go to page 49.

In Game 1, LeBron was no match for Tim and the Spurs. LeBron failed to make a basket until the fourth quarter, and by the end of the night, he had scored just 14 points on 4-of-16 **shooting**. Meanwhile, Duncan had 24 points, 13 **rebounds**, and 5 **blocks** to help lead San Antonio to an 85-76 victory. Game 2 was more of the same. Tim had 23 points, 8 assists, and 9 rebounds in a 103-92 victory. Still, he and his teammates could not escape being called a bland—even boring—team. The words stung, as former teammate Sean Elliott wrote for *MySA.com* following Game 2:

> **"It just astonishes me when I still see people calling the Spurs boring. . . . [I keep] hearing about Kevin Garnett with all the commercials and the chest-beating, and Timmy Duncan isn't any of that. . . . I mean, really, let's look at it. You have this great**

Cleveland Cavaliers forward LeBron James (left) drives past San Antonio Spurs center Tim Duncan during the Cavaliers 85–76 loss to the Spurs in Game 1 of the NBA Finals, June 7, 2007. Basketball fans looked forward to watching the finals matchup between two of the NBA's biggest stars. But the veteran Duncan kept King James from being crowned an NBA champion, as the Spurs swept Cleveland in four games.

team on the floor, playing ego-less, selfless basket-ball. You have a guy so sound fundamentally that you put taller, more athletic guys on him and he still destroys them. . . . We have an endearing team, with a lot of endearing qualities. And you call it boring?**

⇒ GETTING THE JOB DONE ⇐

"Boring" certainly did not accurately describe Tim's game. As Elliott had written, Tim was not flashy. He didn't talk trash. He just went out and did the job he was supposed to do. He had made a career out of doing this, and he continued to do it in Game 3. With teammate

The Spurs celebrate their 2007 NBA title, with Tim (center) holding up the championship trophy. Next to Tim is San Antonio guard Tony Parker, holding the trophy he received for being selected as the most valuable player in the NBA Finals. Parker's emergence as San Antonio's top scorer allowed Tim to focus on rebounding and defense during the series.

Tony Parker stepping up his game and becoming the go-to guy for baskets, Duncan didn't need to score. He netted 14 points in the third contest—the fewest he had ever scored in an NBA Finals game—but contributed 9 rebounds, 3 assists, and 2 blocked shots in the 75-72 victory.

Likewise, in Game 4, Duncan focused less on scoring and more on leading in other ways, scoring just 12 points but snagging 15 rebounds on the evening. Meanwhile, Parker scored 24 and Manu Ginobili added 27 as the Spurs completed the sweep, squeaking past Cleveland, 83-82. Parker, not Duncan, was named the Finals MVP, but for a player like Duncan, who cherished team success above all else in basketball, that didn't matter. He and his teammates were the best team in pro basketball once again, and that was enough. As Tim told Tom Withers of the Associated Press afterwards:

> **It never gets old, it never gets old. Unbelievable. Such a great run, a great journey, a great bunch of guys. . . . This one's sweeter. The road that we took to get here was as tough as we ever had it. Guys persevered, we had great performances from [players] one to 12.**

Tim has called San Antonio's 2007 title the sweetest of his career, because of the way that the Spurs had worked together to overcome obstacles as a team. It may seem out of character for a star athlete to think that way, but that's Tim Duncan. You might call Tim quiet, boring, or blue collar. But there is another thing you have to call him—a champion, four times over.

Tim Duncan grew up on St. Croix, a Caribbean island that is a territory of the United States. Although he is an NBA star, Tim has not forgotten his roots. Through his charitable foundation, Tim has provided money for a hospital and for the island's first basketball court. Here, Tim hugs his father, William.

A Bittersweet Road to Stardom

TIMOTHY THEODORE DUNCAN, THE YOUNGEST child of William and Ione Duncan, was born on April 25, 1976, in Christiansted, St. Croix, in the U.S. Virgin Islands. Duncan was the couple's third child, joining sisters Cheryl and Tricia. His father was a successful **mason**, while his mother worked as a **midwife** on the island.

CROSS-CURRENTS

If you would like to learn more about Tim Duncan's island home, check out "St. Croix, U.S. Virgin Islands." Go to page 50. ▶▶

Tim was a very intelligent child, and his grades were so impressive that, at the age of eight, he was able to skip the third grade entirely and advance to the fourth grade in school. He was a big fan of superheroes growing up and had a collection of comic books that were his prize possessions. Still, it was athletic competition that brought him the most joy, and Tim was a natural athlete.

All three Duncan children were talented swimmers. At the age of 14, Tim's sister Tricia qualified for the 1988 Summer Olympics in the backstroke. Tim was, according to all accounts, even more gifted in the water than his big sister. He trained along with his sisters, and by the age of 13, he was becoming dominant in the 400-meter freestyle event. Tim was so successful that many people, including Tricia, thought that he could have been a medalist at the 1992 Olympics. However, he would never have the chance to find out.

TRAGIC LOSSES AND MONUMENTAL GAINS

The summer of 1989 brought a series of events that would change Tim's life forever. First, his mother Ione was diagnosed with breast cancer. She began treatments immediately and was still undergoing them in September of that year when Hurricane Hugo crashed into the isle of St. Croix. Hugo destroyed or damaged homes, buildings, and other facilities throughout the island—including the pool that the Duncan family had used for training and the hospital facilities where Ione was being treated.

During the chaos that followed, Ione's treatment was disrupted. She died on April 24, 1990, just one day before Tim's 14th birthday. For Tim, who has called his mother the biggest influence on his life, the loss was devastating. However, his father later told Associated Press sportswriter Chip Brown that Tim never let others know that he was hurting:

CROSS-CURRENTS

For more information about one of the most devastating storms in U.S. history, read "Hurricane Hugo." Go to page 50. ▶▶

> **❝Tim never had much of a reaction to anything, including the death of his mother. . . . Different people have different ways of showing grief or joy. Tim just moves on gracefully.❞**

The water on the island had been declared too full of bacteria for safe swimming after Hurricane Hugo. Added to the death of his mother, the loss of his training facility spelled the end of Tim's Olympic swimming aspirations. Desperate for some other way to fill his time, Tim turned to an old gift he had received from sister Cheryl

ST. CROIX
Battered Island Welcomes Troops, Aid

By Ron Howell
Newsday Staff Correspondent

Christiansted, St. Croix, Virgin Islands — A measure of calm returned to this battered island yesterday as the last contingents of 1,100 U.S. soldiers and agents arrived to patrol the streets.

The troops, some armed with machine guns and others with M-16 rifles, took up positions mainly in the downtown area. From time to time relieved island residents would shout welcoming remarks from a passing car.

"I hope they bring a thousand more of you guys down here. It's a beautiful sight," yelled L. Flores, a laundromat owner who said he stayed home all week with a firearm handy so he could protect his wife and family from looters.

Though many welcomed the armed presence of the soldiers and FBI agents, the lawlessness that reigned earlier in the week probably ended because there virtually was nothing left to steal from the stores.

In the wake of Hurricane Hugo's assault Sunday, crowds broke into local businesses and helped themselves to items ranging from clothes to coin-operated washing machines.

Merchants and homeowners were fearful that the residential communities of the middle class would become the next targets. President George Bush on Wednesday ordered in the troops, FBI agents and federal marshals to restore order in the U.S. territory.

Yesterday, there was little sign of tension in the

AFTERMATH on Page 12

Newsday / John Keating

Hugh Cox looks through what is left of his kitchen in St. Croix

A newspaper reports on the situation in St. Croix after Hurricane Hugo battered the island. The Category 5 storm, with winds in excess of 155 miles per hour, hit St. Croix on September 17, 1989. The Duncan family's home was badly damaged. Tim later said that electrical service to the house was not restored for six months.

and her husband, a former college basketball player named Rick Lowery. It was a basketball hoop. New to the game, Tim struggled at first, but he got better quickly. As a freshman, he joined the St. Dunstan's Episcopal High School team, always improving his game as he grew to be seven feet tall. His height and exceptional play caught the attention of many NCAA coaches, including Dave Odom of Wake Forest.

 BIG MAN ON CAMPUS

Duncan enrolled at Wake Forest in 1993 and immediately contributed to the team. As a freshman, he set a school record by blocking 124 shots. The next season, his play improved immensely, as he

TIM DUNCAN

Tim starred at Wake Forest University for four years. While he was at the school, the Demon Deacons won more than 75 percent of their games and reached the NCAA Tournament every year. As a senior, Tim won both the John Wooden Award and the Naismith Award. These are given annually to the top college basketball player in the country.

averaged nearly 17 points per game and helped the Demon Deacons win their first Atlantic Coast Conference (ACC) title in more than three decades. Wake Forest would repeat as ACC champs in Tim's junior year, and Duncan caught the eye of more than one NBA scout by upping his scoring average to 19.1 points per contest.

Some experts believed that he was going to leave school early to join the pros, but that wasn't something Tim had ever seriously considered. He was studying psychology and wanted to earn his degree. But that wasn't the only reason, he told *Stack Magazine*:

CROSS-CURRENTS

To learn about history of the school that Tim Duncan attended, check out "Wake Forest University." Go to page 51. ▶▶

> **❝I enjoyed college, I really did. It is great to be in a situation like that, where you have the opportunity to really grow as a person. I was really excited to stay four years and finish up my degree. I got it done so that I could move on and never have to look back later in life and think, 'Now I have to finish [my degree].' It all worked out for me, and I am thankful I did it that way. ❞**

Another reason Tim wanted to return was that he was in a serious relationship. He was dating Amy Sherrill, a fellow Wake Forest student who was studying to become a doctor.

Coach Odom and Tim's teammates were certainly happy that he stayed with the school. As a senior in 1996–1997, Tim led the Demon Deacons to a 24-7 record, averaging more than 20 points and 14 rebounds a game. However, Tim's Wake Forest career ended on a disappointing note, as the team lost to Stanford in the second round of the NCAA Tourney.

Tim Duncan finished his college career with impressive statistics. He became the first player in NCAA history to tally more than 1,500 points, 1,000 rebounds, 400 blocks, and 200 assists in his career. He was twice named the ACC's Player of the Year, and was named the NCAA Player of the Year following his senior season. After graduating, Tim was the first player chosen in the 1997 NBA **Draft**. He was ready to turn his attention to the pros.

Tim Duncan is congratulated by NBA Commissioner David Stern as the San Antonio Spurs selected the former Wake Forest center as the No. 1 pick in the NBA Draft, June 25, 1997. As the first player chosen in the 1997 NBA draft, Tim was expected to make an immediate impact. San Antonio had been terrible the previous season, finishing with a 20–62 record. Tim proved to be just what the Spurs needed. The team won 56 games in 1997–98, and Tim was chosen as the NBA's Rookie of the Year.

3

An Immediate Impact

ON OCTOBER 31, 1997, TIM DUNCAN MADE HIS NBA debut against the Denver Nuggets. He played 35 minutes in that game, scoring 15 points and adding 10 rebounds, 2 blocks, and a pair of assists in a 107-96 San Antonio victory. It was both a good start to his professional career and a sign of things to come.

Duncan's arrival in the NBA came with much fanfare. Selected first overall by the Spurs, he was labeled as a "can't miss" prospect in the draft that year. He soon signed a three-year contract with San Antonio worth more than $10 million.

Tim had played both forward and center at Wake Forest, but he would play solely at the **power forward** position in San Antonio, because the Spurs already had one of the best centers in the league, David Robinson. Duncan and Robinson would combine to make a fearsome frontcourt during their first season together, earning the nickname "Twin Towers" and stifling even the great Michael Jordan on defense.

⟫ BUILDING RELATIONSHIPS AS A ROOKIE ⟪

To succeed, Tim knew that he needed to establish a good on-court relationship with David Robinson. In 1997, when Tim arrived in San Antonio, Robinson was a 10-year NBA veteran and seven-time All-Star. That experience, and their similar styles of play, made the man known as "The Admiral" a natural tutor for Tim. As *Sports Illustrated*'s Jack McCallum later wrote:

> **❝**Robinson, a post-up center, and Duncan, a post-up power forward, figuratively *and* literally had to make room for each other, a display of selflessness at which both men shrug their shoulders. 'It was a natural process,' says Duncan. 'When I came in, David was the Man and I was just trying to learn the game, develop under his wing.'**❞**

Duncan had a phenomenal **rookie** year. He played in all 82 games during the 1997–98 season, averaging 21.1 points, 11.9 rebounds, 2.7 assists, and 2.5 blocks per game. He won Rookie of the Month honors every month throughout the season and was chosen the NBA's best rookie when the season ended. He was voted to the All-Star Game and became just the fifth first-year player in the history of the game to be named to the NBA's All-Defensive Second Team.

CROSS-CURRENTS

To find out more about The Admiral, Tim's Spurs teammate and All-Star mentor, read "David Robinson." Go to page 52. ▶▶

While he built a professional relationship with Robinson, off the court Tim worked hard on his relationship with girlfriend Amy Sherrill. They had nearly broken up when Tim was drafted into the NBA. Amy was focused on her medical studies at Wake Forest, and feared that Tim would begin dating other women while playing in the NBA. But Tim was not ready to end their relationship. In a *Sports Illustrated* article, sportswriter S.L. Price described what happened between the two:

> **❝**She knew all about pro ballplayers and the women on their trail. Amy was going to become a doctor. . . . She figured she and Tim were through. But he wouldn't have it. For eight months, throughout his breakout rookie year, he called Amy four,

San Antonio Spurs David Robinson (top) and Tim Duncan (right) go up for a rebound during a 1998 game against the Orlando Magic. Tim had a lot of respect for Robinson, who had been considered one of the best centers in the NBA for nearly a decade. The two players soon learned to work well together on the court.

five times a day—before practice, after practice, the moment he touched down in a new city—showing how much he needed her, sanding down her suspicion until, finally, the path between them was again as smooth as glass. **"**

The awards and accolades that Duncan accumulated during his first season in the NBA were impressive. However, it would be those relationships that he took the time to develop and nurture as a rookie that would pay lasting dividends throughout his life and career. Now, Duncan set to work to improve himself on the **court** in preparation for his second season in the NBA. That effort, too, paid off for the man who would become known as "The Big Fundamental."

⋙ THE FIRST CHAMPIONSHIP ⋘

The start of the 1998–99 season was delayed due to a disagreement between NBA players and team owners. Once the labor issues were settled and play resumed, Tim Duncan was at the top of his game. He played in all 50 games that season and was the only NBA player to rank in the top 10 in scoring, rebounding, blocked shots, and **field goal** percentage. He scored in double figures 48 times and averaged 21.7 points and 11.4 rebounds per game. With Tim and his Twin Towers partner David Robinson leading the way, the Spurs finished with the best record in the NBA and powered over the Minnesota Timberwolves, Los Angeles Lakers, and Houston Rockets to reach the NBA Finals. The Spurs lost just one game on their way to the Western Conference title.

In the Finals San Antonio faced the New York Knicks. While Tim had shared the stage with David Robinson throughout much of the year, he took charge with the title on the line. In Game 1, Tim was nearly unstoppable, scoring 33 points and adding 16 rebounds in an 89-77 Spurs victory. In Game 2, he led the Spurs to their 12th consecutive playoff victory (they had lost to Minnesota in the opening round), scoring 25 points, collecting 15 boards, and blocking a quartet of shots in an 80-67 win. That put San Antonio in control of the series. After losing the next game, the Spurs took Game 4, 96-89 and then put the Knicks away by winning a 78-77 nail-biter in the series' fifth game to clinch San Antonio's first NBA title. To no one's surprise, Tim was named the NBA Finals MVP. Afterwards, as he was using a camcorder to record the postgame celebration, Duncan had this to say to the Associated Press:

❝It's an incredible honor. But all it means is that they're going to come at you harder next time. All you do is get a high off it all summer and come

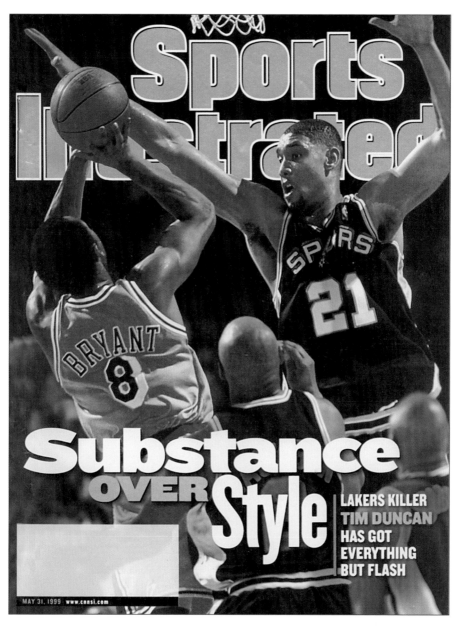

Sports Illustrated

Substance OVER Style

LAKERS KILLER TIM DUNCAN HAS GOT EVERYTHING BUT FLASH

MAY 31, 1999 · www.cnnsi.com

Tim was pictured on the cover of *Sports Illustrated* after the Spurs knocked the Los Angeles Lakers out of the 1999 NBA playoffs. San Antonio went on to win its first NBA championship that season. In 17 playoff games during 1999, Tim averaged 23.2 points, 11.5 rebounds, and 2.7 blocks per game.

back at it next year. . . . It's a blessing to do what we did here, and there's no guarantee we'll ever get back here. **"**

⇒ So Long, San Antonio? ⇐

There was no guarantee that, if Tim Duncan booked a return trip to the NBA Finals, he would be doing so as a member of the San

After averaging 23.2 points and 12.4 rebounds during the 1999–2000 season, Tim agreed to a new contract with San Antonio. "We're all very fortunate to keep him in the fold," said Spurs coach Gregg Popovich. "[We're] thrilled that he's decided to stay with this group of players and coaches and with this city."

Antonio Spurs. The 1999–2000 season was the final year of his contract. After that, other teams would have a chance to bid on Tim's services, and he would certainly be in great demand.

Tim again played exceptional basketball during the 1999–2000 season. He ranked among the top ten players in the NBA in scoring, rebounding, and blocked shots. He was named to the All-Star Game, where he earned co-MVP honors. On March 25, he scored 17 points and added 17 rebounds and a career-high 11 assists against the Cavaliers, making him the first San Antonio player since Robinson in 1994 to post a **triple-double** in a regular season game. Tim again helped lead the Spurs into the playoffs, but a knee injury sidelined him, and San Antonio was eliminated in the first round.

Once the year ended, the 23-year-old Duncan had a tough decision to make. He had enjoyed tremendous success with the Spurs, but the Orlando Magic had come calling with a very lucrative offer. According to some reports, the Magic had offered Duncan a six-year contract worth more than $67 million. While Tim quietly weighed his choices, various media outlets reported that he was leaning toward leaving the Spurs (which Tim later confirmed was true). David Robinson, fearing the loss of his Twin Towers associate, flew to San Antonio from Hawaii to meet with Tim. He wanted to convince Tim to stay so that the duo could continue to work together and earn a second NBA championship.

David's appeal worked, and in August of 2000 Tim signed a $32.6 million deal to remain with San Antonio for the next three seasons. When the Spurs took the floor for their first game of the 2000–01 season, Tim was right there with them. The Spurs' investment in him immediately proved wise: Duncan started all 82 games during the season, averaging 22.2 points, 12.2 rebounds, 3.0 assists, and 2.34 blocked shots in each of those contests. He was named to his third consecutive All-Star Game.

Once again, however, the Spurs faltered in the postseason. They were swept by the Lakers in the Conference finals. This time many people blamed Tim for the disappointing postseason series loss. Although he had scored 40 points in a game earlier in the series with the Lakers, in the final game Tim missed 11 of the 14 shots he took. Fans accused the Spurs star of vanishing when his team needed him most.

⋙ A BUSY OFF-SEASON ⋘

It was an embarrassing defeat, and the loss to the Lakers, as well as the criticism he received for his play during that series, stuck with Duncan during the off-season. But Tim had other matters on his mind. Following the conclusion of the 2000–01 season, he married his longtime girlfriend Amy.

The newlyweds soon established the Tim Duncan Foundation, a charitable organization that would help provide programs in education, youth sports, health, and recreation. The organization was an immediate success, thanks largely to all the hard work the Duncans put into it. On his official Web site, Duncan credited his late mother Ione as being the inspiration for his generosity:

SlamDuncan.com is the official Web site of the Tim Duncan Foundation. The basketball star established the charitable organization in 2001. According to the Web site, "To date, the Tim Duncan Foundation has raised over $650,000 to support its mission by supporting non-profit organizations and programs in South Texas, U.S. Virgin Islands, and in North Carolina."

"When I was a kid my mom used to have us recite this nursery rhyme before bed: 'Good, Better, Best. Never let it rest, until your Good is Better, and your Better is your Best. . . .' We believe that it is our duty to give back to our community and thought a character program was perfect to give kids today the tools to succeed in life."

The rhyme that drove Tim's desire to give back to his community applied equally to his dedication to improve on the court. He had suffered through two straight disappointing playoff performances following his first taste of championship glory, and he had become the target of accusations that he let his teammates down during the playoffs. So that off-season, Tim worked hard to become an even better player than before. Tim would soon prove that his best was yet to come.

During the 2001–02 season, Tim Duncan emerged as the NBA's best player. He averaged a career-best 25.5 points per game and pulled down 12.7 rebounds per game. As a result, Tim was named the league's Most Valuable Player that season. He repeated this accomplishment in 2002–03—a season in which Tim led the Spurs to their second championship.

4

Taking Charge

TIM DUNCAN WAS A MAN ON A MISSION IN October and November of 2001. He was already recognized as one of the better players in the NBA, and had enjoyed both personal and team glory with the San Antonio Spurs. Yet back-to-back playoff embarrassments at the hands of the Los Angeles Lakers motivated him as the 2001–02 season began.

Tim posted a **double-double** in each of his first seven games that season. He scored at least 20 points in five of them, including 33 points against the Charlotte Hornets on November 8. He scored 30 points three more times before the end of the month, and pulled down at least 10 rebounds in 17 of his first 20 games. With his Twin Tower teammate David Robinson showing signs of age and wear, Tim had begun to elevate his game to the next level. He would continue to dominate throughout the season.

⇒ FOCUSED ON THE GOAL ⇐

Tim put together a season for the ages in 2001–02. He became only the 14th player in league history to finish with 2,000 points and 1,000 rebounds in a season, and was the first forward since the 1970s to accomplish the feat. He was fifth in the NBA in scoring, averaging 25.5 points per game. He led the league with 67 double-doubles. His 12.7 rebounds per game were the second best in the NBA, and he was third with 2.48 blocked shots per contest. The Spurs finished with a 58-24 record, winning the Western Conference and returning to the playoffs yet again.

With the Admiral struggling and seeing less time on the court, Tim had carried the team on his back and was named the league's Most Valuable Player. That honor did not come without some controversy, however, as many felt New Jersey Nets guard Jason Kidd was more worthy of the award. Although Kidd did have a good season, he also had shot just 39 percent on the year and averaged a mere 14.1 points per game. Conversely, as Sam Smith of Tribune News Services wrote:

> **"Duncan was better than ever. His free-throw shooting went from 61.8 percent to 79.9 percent. He achieved career highs in points, rebounds and assists, at a time when his teammates weren't as effective as before. He had the second-best shooting percentage of his career and was a runaway leader in double doubles. . . . He was more aggressive and animated on the court than ever, taking a leadership role."**

⇒ AN ALL-TOO-FAMILIAR OUTCOME ⇐

Winning the MVP award was a tremendous honor, no doubt about it, but it was not Tim's ultimate goal for the 2001–02 season. So when the Spurs opened the playoffs against the Seattle Super-Sonics on April 20, 2002, Tim exploded with the best playoff performance of his career: 21 points, 10 rebounds, 11 assists, five blocks, and a perfect seven-for-seven performance at the **free throw** line in a 110-89 San Antonio victory. As Sean Deveney of *The Sporting News* reported:

Tim goes for a shot against Minnesota star Kevin Garnett during a 2002 game. As the Spurs' best player, Tim draws most of the attention from opposing teams. He relishes the challenge. "It's fun to play against him," Duncan once said of Garnett. "He's an incredible player, and he comes out with energy every night."

❝Seattle repeatedly sent three defenders at Duncan in the post. Duncan responded by zipping passes to his wide-open teammates and finished with . . . a triple-double in a blowout win. . . . It's just a step toward redemption. . . . Make no mistake, Duncan is driven. He has not forgotten how last year ended. . . . 'Embarrassing,' Duncan says. 'Call it what you want, it can't happen again.'❞

During the 2002 NBA playoffs, Tim averaged 27.6 points, 14.4 rebounds, and 5 assists per game. Here, he puts up a shot during a playoff game against the Seattle SuperSonics. However, even Tim's spectacular play could not prevent the Spurs from losing to the powerful Los Angeles Lakers in the Western Conference semifinals.

San Antonio would defeat the SuperSonics, although the Spurs needed five games to do so. Tim was fantastic throughout the series, scoring 32 points and adding 12 boards in Game 2, 27 points and 13 rebounds in Game 3, and then 26 points and 21 rebounds in the decisive fifth game. That set the stage for a rematch with the Los Angeles Lakers and a chance for Tim and his San Antonio teammates to avenge their defeat in the previous postseason. It was not to be, however. Despite his determination, Tim and the Spurs simply could not overcome Shaquille O'Neal, Kobe Bryant, and the Lakers. San Antonio fell yet again, four games to one, as L.A. went on to win the NBA championship. It was a bitter end to what had been an incredible year for Tim Duncan.

A NEW AND IMPROVED TIM DUNCAN

Despite the disheartening outcome, observers noticed that Tim Duncan was undergoing a radical change. He had entered the league as a quiet, shy, young man. Since then he had won an NBA title and numerous personal accolades, gotten married, and started a charitable foundation. Thanks to his experiences, as well as the influence of his mentor Robinson, he was becoming a true vocal leader, both in the Spurs locker room and on the court. Never had that become more apparent than in the 2002 playoffs. Tim had lost his father to cancer during the series against Seattle, but he was there for his teammates and played on despite his heavy heart. As Deveney noted:

> **A new Duncan has emerged. For the first four years of his career, he was the Mount Rushmore superstar—quiet, stoic and uncontroversial. He typically racked up 20-point, 10-rebound nights and left the Spurs' talking to veteran jaw-flapper Avery Johnson, who was known for needling his teammates when they were not playing up to standards. But when Johnson left for Denver last summer as a free agent, Duncan recognized a void in verbality and nominated himself to fill it. . . . 'I had to' Duncan says. 'I just see it as part of my job and part of being a leader.'**

The growth process continued during the 2002–03 season, which would be Robinson's last in the NBA. Tim again had a phenomenal year. He averaged 23.3 points, 12.9 rebounds, 3.9 assists, and 2.93 blocked shots in 81 regular-season games. Duncan was the only player in the entire league to rank in the top 10 in scoring, rebounds, blocks, and field goal percentage. Tim led San Antonio to the best record in the NBA, which gave the team home-court advantage throughout the postseason. He was named to the All-Star Game and earned All-NBA First Team honors and All-Defensive First Team honors. Tim also was named the league's Most Valuable Player for the second straight season. He became just the eighth player to accomplish that feat, and the first since Michael Jordan a decade earlier.

CROSS-CURRENTS

To learn more about the last player to win back-to-back MVP awards before Tim Duncan, read "Michael Jordan." Go to page 53. ▶▶

⇒ FINALLY, A CHAMPION AGAIN ⇐

It had been a good year, but it would not be a great year if the Spurs faltered in the playoffs again. Tim was not about to let that happen. The Spurs knocked off the Phoenix Suns in the opening round and then prepared to face their foils from previous seasons, the Los Angeles Lakers. This time, the outcome would be different. Tim led the Spurs over L.A. in six games, and then past the Dallas Mavericks in seven.

At long last, Tim and his teammates were back in the NBA Finals. Opposing them would be Jason Kidd and the New Jersey Nets. It promised to be a hard-fought battle, but Tim Duncan simply would not be denied. In Game 1, he scored 32 points and collected 20 rebounds in a 101-89 San Antonio victory. Kidd and the Nets came roaring back to win the next game. After the first four games of the 2003 Finals, the teams were deadlocked at two games apiece.

At this point, Tim Duncan took over. He had 29 points and 17 rebounds in a 93-83 victory in Game 5, and followed that with one of the greatest games in NBA Finals history—21 points, 20 rebounds, 10 assists, and 8 blocked shots, a near quadruple-double—to close out the series in Game 6.

The Spurs were once again NBA champions. Tim had averaged 24.2 points, 17.0 rebounds, 5.3 assists, and an NBA Finals–record 5.3 blocks per game. For the second time, he was named the MVP of the championship series. He had become just the ninth player in NBA history to complete the trifecta, winning a regular-season

Tim Duncan poses with his second MVP trophy. He won the award at the end of the 2002–03 regular season. During that season Tim was among the league leaders in scoring (seventh, 23.3 points per game), rebounding (third, 12.9 rebounds per game), and blocked shots (third, 2.9 blocks per game).

MVP award, NBA championship, and the Finals MVP all in the same season. Yet, while he and his team had won so much during the season, as Game 6 came to a close, and with it the 2002–03 NBA season, no one could forget that San Antonio was also about to suffer a major loss—David Robinson.

CROSS-CURRENTS

For info on the first player to win the NBA's MVP and the Finals MVP in the same season, read "Willis Reed." Go to page 54. ▶▶

President George W. Bush welcomed the Spurs to the White House Rose Garden on October 14, 2003. At the ceremony, President Bush praised Tim's team-first approach to winning: "It's a phenomenal tribute to the San Antonio Spurs that they've got such great individual players who are willing to work as a team. And it's a wonderful example for our country."

⟫ LIFE WITHOUT THE ADMIRAL ⟪

Even though Robinson's role on the team had been steadily declining, things would be vastly different for Tim without the Admiral around. Robinson had helped his protégé develop his skills on the court. He had advised Tim on contract matters. The two had also become fast friends, sharing a love of many things, including video games. During the team's June 15 press conference, just minutes after his team's victory over the Nets, Tim was asked what it would feel like playing basketball the following season without David Robinson. He responded:

> **❝Dave's been an incredible part of this team for a lot of years. I can't even imagine, honestly. For a second there on the court, last couple seconds, I really thought, 'You know what, I'm not gonna play with this guy again. I'm gonna have to come out on this court without him. It's gonna be weird.' I don't know what to expect. . . . We'll fill a void and we'll find a way to hopefully get back here.❞**

Filling that void would prove to be a tall task indeed. During the 2003–04 season, Tim once again posted solid numbers, averaging 22.3 points, 12.4 rebounds, 3.1 assists, and 2.68 blocks per game en route to earning All-NBA and All-Defensive Team honors for the seventh straight season. The only other player to do that had been David Robinson himself.

Yet although San Antonio had won 57 regular-season games, Tim had been unable to lead the Spurs to a second consecutive NBA title. There was little doubt that Tim Duncan had become one of the NBA's elite players. But could he win a title now that the Twin Towers were no more?

When David Robinson retired after the Spurs' championship season of 2002–03, Tim Duncan was thrust into the role of team leader. Tim quickly proved up to the task. He led the team back to the playoffs in each of the next two seasons. In 2004–05 Tim and the Spurs won a third NBA title.

5

Cementing His Legacy

THE SAN ANTONIO SPURS HAD A NUMBER OF very good players on the roster, such as guards Tony Parker and Emanuel "Manu" Ginobili. However, with David Robinson retired, it had become clear that the Spurs were Tim Duncan's team. All eyes were on him. Win or lose, the pressure was on Tim.

Tim had assumed this leadership role over several seasons, as Robinson gradually became less of a factor on the **hardwood**. Now, younger players like Parker and Ginobili expected Tim to lead the way, to mentor them the way the Admiral had mentored him in the early days of his career. This wasn't always easy, especially when it came to getting the most out of Parker. As *The Sporting News* reported:

" Duncan plays a stern older brother role to Parker. . . . showing patience with the rookie without *being too soft on him. Duncan understands Parker is young, but Duncan also understands that one of his duties. . . . is to prod young players. . . . Early this season, Duncan got frustrated with Parker—the new kid was undergoing growing pains at a time when Duncan wanted to focus on winning.* 99

There may have been some growing pains, but it would all come together in the end. In 2004–05, Parker had the best year of his career, averaging 16.6 points and 6.1 assists a game. Ginobili was voted to the All-Star Game after he averaged 16 points and shot over 47 percent from the floor and nearly 38 percent from three-point range during the season. And Tim Duncan? Despite battling injuries all year long, he appeared in 66 games and averaged 20.3 points and 11.1 rebounds per game. Tim made nearly 50 percent of his shots from the field. He scored at least 20 points at 34 different times, was the only player in the league named to both the All-NBA First Team and the All-Defensive First Team, and joined Ginobili in the All-Star Game. Together, they led the Spurs to 59 wins, another Southwest Division title, and a trip to the NBA playoffs.

⇒ A TITLE OF HIS VERY OWN ⇐

The Spurs opened the 2005 playoffs against the Denver Nuggets and came out sluggish in Game 1. Tim only connected on seven of the 22 shots he took from the floor, and the Spurs dropped the opening game. Nobody panicked, however, and San Antonio battled back to win the next four games to advance to the Western Conference semifinals. Next up were the SuperSonics, who took Tim and the Spurs to six games before bowing out. The Spurs then beat the Suns, four games to one, in the Western Conference Finals to reach the championship round for the third time in Tim's career.

Now Tim Duncan had a chance to prove that he could win an NBA Championship without the Admiral. But standing in San Antonio's way were the defending NBA champions, the Detroit Pistons. The Spurs won the first game, 84-69, with Tim scoring 24 points and adding 17 rebounds. In the second game, it was Ginobili who contributed the most, scoring 27 points and adding 7 assists in a 97-76 Spurs victory. After Detroit took Game 3, the Spurs won the fourth game to put the Pistons on the edge of

Tim provided advice and guidance to the younger San Antonio players, particularly talented point guard, Tony Parker (number 9). Within a few years, the young French guard had become one of the best players in the league. Parker was a major part of the Spurs' run to a third championship in 2004–05.

As the Spurs moved through the 2005 playoffs, Tim did whatever it took for his team to win. Here, Tim looks to pass the ball to a teammate during a 2005 Western Conference Finals game against the Phoenix Suns. In 23 playoff games that year, Tim averaged 23.6 points and 12.4 rebounds a game.

elimination. Detroit took the series to the limit, however, winning the next two games to force a decisive seventh game.

The Pistons seemed to have momentum on their side. Tim and the Spurs had struggled in the fourth quarter of the fifth and sixth games of the series. Once again, Tim found his ability to lead being questioned by fans and the press.

Tim answered his critics in Game 7. With the Spurs down by three points late in the third quarter, he went on a tear. Tim scored 12 points and snagged 6 rebounds during the final period, motivating his team and leading San Antonio to a come-from-behind 81-74 victory. The Spurs had won their third NBA title. Tim finished the seventh game with 25 points and 11 rebounds, winning Finals MVP honors for his clutch performance. Former Spurs great George Gervin later talked about Duncan's performance in Game 7, with the title on the line:

> **In the third quarter, 'Mr. MVP' Tim Duncan took over. Once he started getting assertive, everyone else was motivated . . . he showed the guys he was there to play. He just knows how to win. A lot of people were talking about how soft he is and how he needs to do this and he needs to do that—all he needs to do is be Tim Duncan. He has answered all of the critics who were making all that noise and questioning his ability and his assertiveness.**

⟫ IN RARE COMPANY ⟪

Duncan's third championship put him in elite company. As the only member of the 2005 team who had also been on the Spurs roster when they won their first NBA title in 1999, Tim had won championships with the same team, but with two completely different supporting casts. It was an amazing feat that had only been accomplished once before, by former Boston Celtics center Bill Russell, a basketball Hall of Famer.

Duncan also became just the fourth player to win at least three NBA Finals MVP awards, joining Magic Johnson, Michael Jordan, and Shaquille O'Neal in that exclusive fraternity. Tim's legacy could already stand alongside any of the greats who had played the game,

Throughout his career, Tim has often been compared to Shaquille O'Neal (pictured). Both Tim and Shaq are among the most dominant players of their era offensively and defensively. Each has won four NBA championships. In 2003, Shaq gave Tim the nickname "The Big Fundamental" out of respect for Tim's solid all-around play on the court.

as author John Hareas observed in his book *One Team. One Goal. Mission Accomplished: The 2005 NBA Champion San Antonio Spurs*:

> "His basketball legacy is far from complete. Not at the age of 29, when he is in the prime of his career and has three NBA championships and three Finals MVPs on his résumé. When Tim Duncan retires, ultimately, he will be judged not on his unassuming nature, stoic demeanor or the fact that he doesn't provide reporters great sound bites, but rather he'll be evaluated by the number of championships his teams have won. Like all legends are."

Whether or not Duncan was considered a legend in the eyes of most people, he certainly had been playing like one, and he would continue to do so during the next couple of seasons.

Despite being hobbled by a foot injury during the 2005–06 season, Tim averaged 18.6 points, 11.0 rebounds, 3.2 assists and 2.03 blocks. He was voted into the 2006 All-Star Game, and on November 7, he recorded the 1,500th blocked shot of his career. The Spurs could not defend their NBA title, however, falling in the playoffs to the Dallas Mavericks.

In 2006–07, Tim again took home All-NBA, All-Defensive Team and All-Star honors. He scored his 15,000th career point in a game against the Seattle SuperSonics on November 26. Tim appeared in 80 games for the Spurs during the regular season, averaging 20 points and 10.6 rebounds. In the playoffs, Tim scored in double figures in every Spurs game as the team won its fourth NBA title.

CROSS-CURRENTS

To more about another one of the greatest players in Spurs history, check out "George Gervin." Go to page 54. ▶▶

⚞ DISAPPOINTMENT IN 2008 ⚟

The Spurs started the 2007–08 season just as they had ended the previous year. San Antonio won 14 of its first 17 games. The team finished with a 56-26 record. This was the ninth straight season in which the Spurs had won at least 50 games.

In the team's first game of the 2008 NBA playoffs, Tim led all scorers with 40 points as the Spurs defeated the Phoenix Suns in

In 2006, Tim was joined on the Western Conference All-Star Team by his Spurs' teammate, Tony Parker. Pictured are (front, left to right) Parker, Steve Nash, Ray Allen (back, left to right) Shawn Marion, Elton Brand, Kevin Garnett, Dirk Nowitzki, Yao Ming, Pau Gasol, Duncan, Tracy McGrady, and Kobe Bryant.

double overtime, 117-115. Tim continued to play well as San Antonio won the playoff series against Phoenix in five games.

In the Western Conference semifinals, San Antonio faced the New Orleans Hornets. In the first two games, the Spurs looked outclassed. New Orleans won both games easily, 101-82 and 102-84. However, the Spurs turned things around with a win in Game 3. In Game 4, Tim scored 22 points and pulled down 15 rebounds as San Antonio won to tie the series. The Spurs went on to win the series in seven games, and advanced to the Western Conference finals.

In the conference finals, the Spurs faced their longtime rivals, the Los Angeles Lakers. Although Tim scored a game-high 30 points and pulled down 18 rebounds in the first game, the Lakers prevailed, 89-85. Los Angeles went on to win the series in five games.

Tim was disappointed that the Spurs were not able to defend their NBA title:

> **"Just got to gear it up again to go to next year. Love what we had this year. We just weren't good enough through stretches."**

Tim waits for a pass from Tony Parker during a 2008 game against the Los Angeles Clippers. Tim had another solid season in 2007–08. He appeared in 78 games and averaged 19.3 points, 11.3 rebounds, and 1.9 blocked shots per game. The Spurs were unable to defend their NBA title, however, losing in the Western Conference Finals.

⪼ THE BEST POWER FORWARD EVER? ⪻

Tim has played more than 800 regular-season games in the NBA. He has scored nearly 18,000 career points, collected close to 10,000 rebounds, and blocked nearly 2,000 shots to date. He has won four league championships with the Spurs, and on three occasions was named the Most Valuable Player of the NBA Finals. He was been

"Duncan has become arguably the best power forward of all time . . . and he just keeps getting better," writes former coach Jack Ramsay, a member of the basketball hall of fame. "He . . . can score . . . with turnaround jumpers, jump hooks, and quick drop-step moves. He makes strong defenders back off him."

named the NBA regular season MVP twice. He has been to the All-Star Game on 10 occasions and is also a 10-time All-NBA performer. Without a doubt, Tim Duncan's résumé is most impressive, leading some to call him the greatest power forward to ever play the game.

Former teammate and longtime mentor David Robinson once told *USA Today* reporter David DuPree:

> **"**No question he's the greatest power forward ever. It's hard to compare anyone to Tim. He's in a class by himself. He's been consistently good for so long, and he's been ridiculous from Day One. He's just a steady presence, and the team feeds off it. . . . He's one person who impacts every single aspect of the game. Everything you ask him to do he's able to do.**"**

Robinson is not alone in this assessment of Tim. The Association for Professional Basketball Research has named Tim one of the 100 Greatest Professional Basketball Players of the 20th Century.

Speculation has begun about when Tim Duncan will step away from the game and what the future will hold when he does. He and his wife Amy now have a daughter and a son to raise. And he is dedicated to his charitable work, especially making sure the Tim Duncan Foundation continues to benefit the children of San Antonio, Winston-Salem, and St. Croix. He has talked about starting his own business, or getting into coaching. For now, though, Tim Duncan remains a basketball player. Judging by his career to date, he will be remembered as one of the best the game has ever seen.

The San Antonio Spurs

The San Antonio Spurs were founded in 1967, but the team wasn't originally called by that name. It was known as the Dallas Chaparrals, and it played in the American Basketball Association (ABA). In the team's first year, Dallas won 46 of 78 games and reached the **playoffs**. Yet, despite this initial success, the franchise would eventually find itself in dire straits. The team began to struggle, and fan interest plummeted. Attempts to turn the Chaparrals into a touring team, playing games at different cities throughout Texas, couldn't recapture the fans' attention. Eventually, the franchise was sold and moved to San Antonio. In 1973, the team was renamed the Spurs.

San Antonio never won a title in the ABA. In 1976, when the ABA folded, the Spurs were absorbed into the National Basketball Association (NBA) along with four other clubs. San Antonio won its first NBA game, beating Philadelphia by three points on October 22, 1976. As the Chaparrals and the Spurs, the franchise has won over 1,500 ABA and NBA games.

The Spurs reached the playoffs in their first season, and several times after that, but were unable to win a league championship until 1999— Tim Duncan's second season with the team. Since then, the Spurs have won championships in 2003, 2005, and 2007. (Go back to page 6.) ◀◀

Fans stand to watch on-court activities during a Spurs home game. Since Tim Duncan joined the team, the Spurs have been the NBA's most successful franchise. San Antonio has made the playoffs every season that Duncan has been with the team. The Spurs have won four NBA championships since 1997–98, more than any other team in that time.

Bill Russell

While Tim Duncan's four NBA championships are impressive, he has a way to go to catch up with the great Bill Russell. A basketball Hall of Famer who played center with the Boston Celtics during the 1950s and 1960s, Russell won 11 NBA titles during his career.

William Felton Russell was born on February 12, 1934, in Monroe, Louisiana. He played college ball at San Francisco before being drafted into the NBA. In Boston, Russell would become the cornerstone of a basketball dynasty. While leading the Celtics to 11 titles in 13 seasons, Russell was named the league's Most Valuable Player five times and was a 12-time NBA All-Star.

Russell was a tremendous defensive player, known for blocking shots and grabbing rebounds. He once collected 51 **boards** in a single game. He finished his career with over 14,500 points, 21,600 rebounds, and 4,100 assists in nearly 1,000 career games. When he retired after the 1968–69 season, Russell was second all-time in career rebounds. He also was the first African American to coach an NBA team, serving as player-coach of the Celtics from 1966 to 1969 and later coaching two other teams.

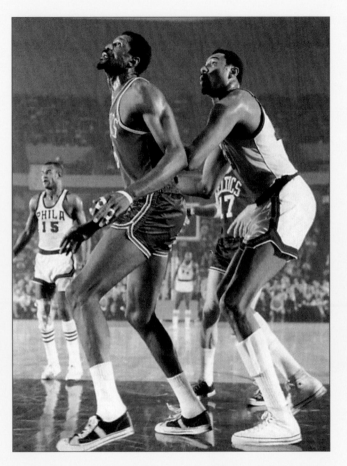

During his career Boston Celtics center Bill Russell (left, wearing green jersey) waged many great battles against another legendary center, Philadelphia's Wilt Chamberlain (right). Russell was one of the greatest players in NBA history. He won the league's MVP award five times. More importantly, Russell helped his team win the NBA title 11 times.

In 1975, Russell became the first black player voted into the Basketball Hall of Fame. In 1996, he was named one of the 50 Greatest Players in NBA History.

(Go back to page 6.)

St. Croix, U.S. Virgin Islands

Along with St. Thomas and St. John, Tim Duncan's home of St. Croix is one of the three islands making up the United States Virgin Islands, a U.S. territory in the Caribbean, east of Puerto Rico. The Virgin Islands are roughly twice the size of Washington, D.C., and enjoy a **subtropical** climate for most of the year, with a rainy season during the fall months. Hills and mountains dominate the landscape, with very little flat ground. More than 100,000 people live in the territory. While tourism is the top industry, the islands are also known for producing petroleum, making watches, and distilling rum.

St. Croix is the largest of the three Virgin Islands and has belonged to seven different countries since the 15th century. In 1493, thanks to Christopher Columbus, Spain became the first European country to colonize the territory. After that, Great Britain, the Netherlands, France, Malta, and Denmark all laid claim to the land. In the early 20th century, the island became a territory of the United States.

The capital of St. Croix is Christiansted, which is one of just two towns on the island. Christiansted has a population of about 3,000 people. St. Croix as a whole is home to more than 53,000 people, most of whom speak a form of the Creole language known as Crucian.

(Go back to page 11.)

Hurricane Hugo

Tim Duncan's hometown in the Virgin Islands was one of many places devastated by Hurricane Hugo in 1989. Meteorologists—scientists who study the weather—first detected the tropical storm that became Hugo off the coast of Africa on September 9, 1989. In just a few days the storm gained hurricane force. On a scale that scientists use to measure the strength of hurricanes, Hugo was considered a Category 5 hurricane—the most intense and damaging storm. On September 17 and 18, the hurricane passed over St. Croix and the Leeward Islands. Hugo then crossed Puerto Rico and hit the mainland United States at Charleston, South Carolina.

The storm caused immense damage wherever it hit. Hurricane Hugo caused an estimated $7 billion of destruction in the mainland United States, with another $1 billion in the Virgin Islands and Puerto Rico. On St. Croix, power and phone lines were knocked down, hospitals and other structures were left in ruins, and drinking water was contaminated. Many people were left homeless, and looting or rioting became serious concerns. The situation got so out of hand that U.S. military personnel were flown into the island along with medical workers, engineers, and others to help restore order and provide essential care and provisions for those in need. (Go back to page 12.)

Wake Forest University

Wake Forest University, located in Winston-Salem, North Carolina, was founded in 1834 as a private school. Today Wake Forest has an enrollment of 4,300 students. In addition to Tim Duncan, many other alumni have become famous after leaving the school. Notable alumni include former U.S. Senators Jesse Helms and Josiah W. Bailey, actor Carroll O'Connor, golfers Arnold Palmer and Lanny Wadkins, basketball player Chris Paul, and football players Brian Piccolo and Ricky Proehl. The faculty includes Pulitzer Prize–winning poet and civil rights activist Maya Angelou.

The school's athletic teams are called the Demon Deacons, and they play in the Atlantic Coast Conference (ACC). The Demon Deacons have won several championships over the years. Wake Forest's football team has been to eight postseason bowl games, winning five of them, and have twice been ACC conference champions. In men's basketball, Wake Forest won the ACC regular season title in 1960, 1962, 1995, and 2003, and brought home the conference tournament championship in 1961, 1962, 1995, and 1996. Wake Forest has reached the NCAA tournament 20 times, reaching the Final Four once, in 1962. In addition, the Demon Deacons have won national championships in baseball (1955), golf (1974, 1975, 1986) and women's field hockey (2002, 2003, 2004). In all, the school has won eight NCAA titles in four different sports. (Go back to page 15.) ◀◀

Wake Forest students and alumni have a tradition of celebrating athletic victories by covering the trees surrounding the school's historic North Carolina campus with rolls of toilet paper. During Tim's four years at Wake Forest, the men's basketball team won the Atlantic Coast Conference title twice and went to the NCAA Tournament four times.

David Robinson

David Robinson was born on August 6, 1965, in Key West, Florida. He was the second child of Ambrose and Freda Robinson. Because Ambrose was in the U.S. Navy, the family moved many times during David's childhood. After high school, six-foot-seven David decided to enroll at the U.S. Naval Academy. While at the academy, David grew to more than seven feet tall. He soon became a star, and in 1987 was named the college basketball player of the year.

David was drafted by the Spurs in 1987, but could not join the team until the 1989–90 season because he was committed to two years of naval service. His impact on the team was immediate.

In 1990, he became the first Spur chosen as NBA Rookie of the Year. Soon he was one of the league's best players. He appeared in ten All-Star Games and was named the NBA's Most Valuable Player in 1995. "The Admiral," as the former navy serviceman came to be known, scored more than 20,000 points and collected more than 10,000 rebounds in his career. In 1996, he was named one of the NBA's 50 greatest players.

Today, David and his wife Valerie run the David Robinson Foundation, a faith-based organization designed to help support families. They also founded Carver Academy, a school for pre-kindergarten through eighth-grade students in San Antonio. (Go back to page 18.) ◀◀

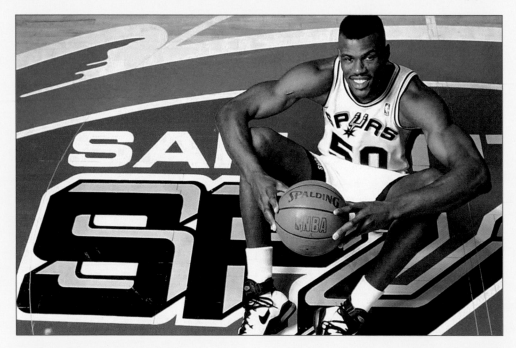

The Spurs' David Robinson is widely considered one of the greatest centers ever to play in the NBA. During a 14-season career, Robinson scored 20,790 points (an average of 21.1 per game) and pulled down 10,497 rebounds (10.6 per game). Robinson won a scoring title in 1993–94, and was selected as the NBA's most valuable player in 1994–95.

Michael Jordan

The last man to win back-to-back MVP awards before Tim Duncan was a guy by the name of Michael Jordan. Jordan should be no stranger to even the most casual of basketball fans. The former Chicago Bulls star is one of the best players in NBA history, if not the greatest of all time.

Michael was born on February 17, 1963, in Brooklyn, New York. He attended the University of North Carolina, where he helped lead the Tar Heels to a national championship in 1982 and won college player of the year honors in 1984. Jordan was drafted by the Bulls in 1984, and was voted Rookie of the Year after the 1984–85 NBA season.

Jordan, who is sometimes known as "MJ" or "Air Jordan," was undoubtedly the dominant player of his era. He was a six-time NBA champion, winning the Finals MVP each time, and was the league's MVP five times (1988, 1991, 1992, 1996, and 1998). He was a 10-time All-NBA first team selection, a 14-time All-Star, and a three-time All-Star Game MVP. He won an NBA-record 10 scoring titles and retired having scored more than 32,000

"By acclamation, Michael Jordan is the greatest basketball player of all time," notes the NBA's online biography of the Chicago Bulls superstar, who is pictured here in 1996. *"[As] a phenomenal athlete with a unique combination of fundamental soundness, grace, speed, power, artistry, improvisational ability and an unquenchable competitive desire, Jordan single-handedly redefined the NBA superstar."*

points in his career. He was named one of the 50 Greatest Players in NBA History in 1996, and was later named the greatest athlete of the twentieth century by ESPN.

(Go back to page 32.)

Willis Reed

The first person to win the NBA Most Valuable Player and the Finals MVP awards in the same year was Willis Reed, a center who played for the New York Knicks during the 1960s and 1970s. Reed was born on June 25, 1942, in the tiny Louisiana town of Hico. Reed played college ball at Grambling State, leading the school to an NAIA championship and three Southwestern Athletic Conference (SWAC) titles during his career. He was selected by New York in the second round of the 1964 draft, and would go on to win 1965 Rookie of the Year.

Reed's career had many highlights. He was named to All-NBA teams five times and to the All-Star Game on seven occasions. However, he is best known for the 1970 season, when he was named the NBA's Most Valuable Player. He was named Finals MVP after his heroic Game 7 comeback from a leg injury helped spur the Knicks to a 113-99 victory and the league championship. The sight of him hobbling out onto the court remains one of the sport's lasting images.

Reed led New York to another NBA title three years later, once again earning Finals MVP honors. His number, 19, was later retired by the Knicks, and he was inducted into the Basketball Hall of Fame in 1982.

(Go back to page 33.)

George Gervin

George Gervin, known as "The Iceman" for his cool manner on the court, was the first player in San Antonio Spurs history to score more than 15,000 points in his career. Gervin was born on April 27, 1952, in Detroit. He had a tough childhood, growing up in a single-parent family, with his mother forced to work a variety of different jobs to keep food on the table for her six children.

Once almost cut by his high school basketball coach, Gervin went on to become a star. At Eastern Michigan University, he was averaging 29.5 points per game as a sophomore when he was suspended from the squad for hitting another player during a fight. He was expelled from EMU over the incident, and he then entered the world of professional basketball.

After briefly playing in the minor-league Continental Basketball Association (CBA), Gervin signed up with the Virginia Squires of the American Basketball Association in 1972. He played two seasons before joining the Spurs (then also in the ABA) in 1974. Gervin would continue to play for San Antonio after the franchise moved into the NBA in 1976. He won four scoring titles in his first five NBA seasons and was elected to nine straight All-Star Games from 1977 through 1985. Gervin was the first guard in NBA history to lead the league in scoring three years in a row and was named the MVP of the 1980 All-Star Game.

In 1978, Gervin won the scoring title in one of the most remarkable competitions ever, beating David Thompson of the Denver Nuggets by seven-hundredths of a point, 27.22 to 27.15. The contest came down to the last game of each player's regular season. On that day, Thompson scored 73 points, but it wasn't enough to overtake Gervin, who kept his lead by scoring 63 points in a game that San Antonio lost.

Gervin played his last profession season for the Chicago Bulls in 1985–86. His number 44 jersey has been retired by the Spurs, and in 1996, he was enshrined in the Naismith Memorial Basketball Hall of Fame. Gervin scored more than 20,000 points in the NBA, and when his ABA statistics are added, that total increases to 26,595 for his pro career.

(Go back to page 43.) ◀◀

"Iceman" George Gervin became one of San Antonio's biggest stars during the 1970s and 1980s. He won the NBA's scoring title four times, in 1978, 1978, 1980, and 1982. The Spurs have retired Gervin's number, 44, and he remains the team's all-time scoring leader, with 23,602 points in a Spurs uniform.

1976   Timothy Theodore Duncan is born on April 25 in St. Croix, United States Virgin Islands.

1990   At 14 years of age, begins playing basketball.

1994   Enrolls at Wake Forest University.

1995   Helps lead the Demon Deacons to their first ACC title in 33 seasons.

1996   Leads Wake Forest into the Sweet Sixteen and is named ACC Player of the Year.

1997   In his final season in the NCAA, repeats as the ACC Player of the Year and also wins the Naismith College Player of the Year and John Wooden Award; drafted by the San Antonio Spurs with the first overall pick..

1998   Wins NBA Rookie of the Year honors and is also named to the NBA All-Star team.

1999   Helps San Antonio beat the New York Knicks, winning NBA Finals MVP honors as the Spurs win the first NBA championship in team history.

2000   Continues to excel and is not only named to the NBA All-Star Game but is honored as the game's Most Valuable Player.

2001   Marries his girlfriend, Amy Sherrill, and starts the Tim Duncan Foundation.

2002   Named the NBA's Most Valuable Player for the first time in his career.

2003   Becomes just the eighth player in NBA history to win back-to-back MVP awards; leads the Spurs to a second title and is named NBA Finals MVP.

2004   Has another All-Star season in the NBA and wins the bronze medal with the U.S. Olympic Basketball Team.

2005   Wins third NBA Championship with Spurs, as well as third NBA Finals MVP.

2007   With Duncan still at the helm, Spurs win a fourth NBA title.

2008   Named to the Western Conference All-Star Team for the 10th time; leads the Spurs to a 56–26 regular-season record.

Awards and Championships

1996   ACC Player of the Year

1997   ACC Player of the Year, Naismith College Player of the Year, John Wooden Award

1998   NBA Rookie of the Year, All-NBA First Team, NBA All-Star

1999   NBA Champion, NBA Finals MVP, All-NBA First Team

2000   NBA All-Star Game MVP, All-NBA First Team, NBA All-Star

2001   All-NBA First Team, NBA All-Star, Home Team Community Service Award

2002   NBA Most Valuable Player, All-NBA First Team, NBA All-Star

2003   NBA Most Valuable Player, NBA Champion, NBA Finals MVP, All-NBA First Team, NBA All-Star

2004   All-NBA First Team, NBA All-Star, Olympic Bronze Medalist, USA Basketball's Male Athlete of the Year

2005   NBA Champion, NBA Finals MVP, NBA All-Star

2006   NBA All-Star

2007   NBA Champion, NBA All-Star

2008   NBA All-Star

Career Highs

Points—53 vs. Dallas, 12/26/01

Field Goals Made—19 (3 times)

Field Goals Attempted—34

Three Point Field Goals Made—1 (24 times)

Three Point Field Goals Attempted—2 (10 times)

Free Throws Made—17 vs. Utah 01/17/02

Free Throws Attempted—24 vs. Dallas 02/13/01

Offensive Rebounds—12

Defensive Rebounds—23

Total Rebounds—25

Assists—11 vs. Cleveland 03/25/00

Steals—8

Blocks—9 vs. Memphis 01/26/07

Minutes Played—52

Career Statistics

Year	Team	G	GS	MPG	FG%	3P%	FT%	OFF	DEF	RPG	APG	SPG	BPG	TO	PF	PPG
97–98	SAS	82	82	39.1	0.549	0.000	0.662	3.3	8.6	11.9	2.7	0.7	2.5	3.40	3.10	21.1
98–99	SAS	50	50	39.3	0.495	0.143	0.690	3.2	8.2	11.4	2.4	0.9	2.5	2.92	2.90	21.7
99–00	SAS	74	74	38.9	0.490	0.091	0.761	3.5	8.9	12.4	3.2	0.9	2.2	3.27	2.80	23.2
00–01	SAS	82	82	38.7	0.499	0.259	0.618	3.2	9.0	12.2	3.0	0.9	2.3	2.95	3.00	22.2
01–02	SAS	82	82	40.6	0.508	0.100	0.799	3.3	9.4	12.7	3.7	0.7	2.5	3.21	2.60	25.5
02–03	SAS	81	81	39.3	0.513	0.273	0.710	3.2	9.7	12.9	3.9	0.7	2.9	3.06	2.90	23.3
03–04	SAS	69	68	36.6	0.501	0.167	0.599	3.3	9.2	12.4	3.1	0.9	2.7	2.65	2.40	22.3
04–05	SAS	66	66	33.4	0.496	0.333	0.670	3.1	8.0	11.1	2.7	0.7	2.6	1.92	2.20	20.3
05–06	SAS	80	80	34.8	0.484	0.400	0.629	2.9	8.1	11.0	3.2	0.9	2.0	2.48	2.70	18.6
06–07	SAS	80	80	34.1	0.546	0.111	0.637	2.7	7.9	10.6	3.4	0.8	2.4	2.80	2.50	20.0
07–08	SAS	78	78	34.0	0.497	0.000	0.730	3.0	8.3	11.3	2.8	0.7	1.9	2.30	2.40	19.3
Career		824	823	37.2	0.508	0.190	0.684	3.1	8.7	11.8	3.1	0.8	2.4	2.82	2.70	21.6

Career Playoff Statistics

Year	Team	G	GS	MPG	FG%	3P%	FT%	OFF	DEF	RPG	APG	SPG	BPG	TO	PF	PPG
97–98	SAS	9	9	41.6	0.521	0.000	0.667	2.2	6.8	9.0	1.9	0.6	2.6	2.78	2.70	20.7
98–99	SAS	17	17	43.1	0.511	0.000	0.748	3.2	8.2	11.5	2.8	0.8	2.7	3.06	2.90	23.2
00–01	SAS	13	13	40.5	0.488	1.000	0.639	4.2	10.3	14.5	3.8	1.1	2.7	3.85	3.30	24.4
01–02	SAS	9	9	42.2	0.453	0.333	0.822	3.1	11.3	14.4	5.0	0.7	4.3	4.11	2.40	27.6
02–03	SAS	24	24	42.5	0.529	0.000	0.677	4.0	11.4	15.4	5.3	0.6	3.3	3.17	3.30	24.7
03–04	SAS	10	10	40.5	0.522	0.000	0.632	3.3	8.0	11.3	3.2	0.8	2.0	4.20	3.40	22.1
04–05	SAS	23	23	37.8	0.464	0.200	0.717	3.8	8.7	12.4	2.7	0.3	2.3	2.70	2.90	23.6
05–06	SAS	13	13	37.9	0.573	0.000	0.718	2.5	8.0	10.5	3.3	0.9	1.9	2.62	3.80	25.8
06–07	SAS	20	20	36.8	0.521	0.000	0.644	3.7	7.8	11.5	3.3	0.6	3.1	2.95	3.00	22.2
07–08	SAS	17	17	39.2	0.449	0.200	0.626	3.6	10.9	14.5	3.3	0.9	2.1	2.41	2.41	20.2
Career		155	155	40.0	0.501	0.143	0.691	3.5	9.2	12.7	3.3	0.7	2.7	3.08	3.01	23.4

G, GS: games, games started

MPG: minutes played per game

FG%, 3P%, FT%: Field goal shooting percentage, three-point field goal shooting percentage, free throw shooting percentage.

OFF: offensive rebounds per game

DEF: defensive rebounds per game

RPG: total rebounds per game

APG: assists per game

SPG: steals per game

BPG: blocked shots per game

TO: turnovers per game

PF: personal fouls committed per game

PPG: points scored per game

Books

Adams, Sean. *Tim Duncan*. Minneapolis: Lerner Publishing Group. 2004.

Bednar, Chuck. *The San Antonio Spurs*. San Diego: Lucent Books, 2004.

Hareas, John. *One Team. One Goal. Mission Accomplished: The 2005 NBA Champion San Antonio Spurs*. Daytona Beach, FL: EventDay Media, 2005.

LeBoutillier, Nate. *The Story of the San Antonio Spurs*. Mankato, MN: Creative Education, 2006.

Ramsay, Jack. *Dr. Jack's Leadership Lessons Learned from a Lifetime in Basketball*. Hoboken, NJ: John Wiley & Sons, 2004.

Roselius, J. Chris. *Tim Duncan: Champion On and Off the Court*. Berkeley Heights, NJ: Enslow Publishers. 2006.

Stewart, Mark. *The San Antonio Spurs*. Chicago: Norwood House Press, 2006.

Walters, John. *Tim Duncan*. Chanhassen, MN: The Child's World. 2007.

Web Sites

http://www.slamduncan.com
Tim Duncan's official Web site. Includes stats, the latest news about Duncan's career, and tons of information about his life and activities off the court.

http://www.nba.com/spurs/
The official homepage of Tim Duncan's team, the San Antonio Spurs. It includes team news, statistics, the current season's schedule, and much more.

http://wakeforestsports.ocsn.com/
The official Web site of the Wake Forest Demon Deacons, Tim's collegiate team.

http://www.basketball-reference.com/
Basketball-Reference.com, a comprehensive collection of basketball statistics and player information.

http://espn.go.com/
The Internet home of the ESPN television network contains in-depth coverage of a variety of sports, including NBA basketball, as well as detailed information about various athletes and sports teams.

Publisher's note:

The Web sites mentioned in this book were active at the time of publication. The publisher is not responsible for Web sites that have changed their addresses or discontinued operation since the date of publication. The publisher will review and update the Web site addresses each time the book is reprinted.

block—stopping an opposing player's shot with your hand, thus preventing the ball from reaching the basket.

boards—slang term used for rebounds

court—the 94 foot by 50 foot surface on which professional basketball games are played.

double-double—an individual performance in which a player has double-digit numbers in two of the following categories: points, rebounds, assists, steals, or blocked shots.

draft—in sports, the annual process by which teams select new players from the college or amateur ranks, with teams that performed poorly during the past season picking before those with good records.

field goal—a successful shot that is worth two points.

free throw—an uncontested shot given to a player who has been fouled. One shot is awarded for a technical foul, two for a personal foul committed on a player in the act of shooting a two-point shot, and three for fouling a player who is in the act of shooting a three-pointer.

hardwood—another name for a basketball court, so named because of the playing surface traditionally used.

mason—a skilled builder who works with brick, stone, or cement.

midwife—a woman who helps other women in childbirth.

MVP—abbreviation for Most Valuable Player, an award given to a player for exceptional performance during the course of a season, game, or playoff series.

playoffs—a series of games played following the regular season in which the best teams in compete against each other in order to determine a league champion.

power forward—a player who typically plays a role similar to a center in that he plays in the low post on offense and under the basket on defense.

rebound—gaining possession of the basketball following a failed attempted shot, either by a teammate (offensive rebound) or by an opponent (defensive rebound).

rookie—a professional athlete who is playing in his or her first year.

shooting—launching the basketball toward the goal (basket) in order to score points.

shooting percentage—the ratio of successful baskets made by a player or team to the number of shots attempted.

subtropical—adjacent to and similar to the tropics in terms of warm climate and types of storms.

triple-double—an individual performance in which a player has double-digit numbers in three of the following categories: points, rebounds, assists, steals, or blocked shots.

page 6 "It just astonishes me . . ." Sean Elliott, "Sean Elliott: Spurs boring? That's stupid," MySA.com. June 10, 2007. http://blogs.mysanantonio.com/weblogs/elliott/2007/06/sean_elliott_stupid_things.html

page 9 "It never gets old . . ." Quoted in Tom Withers, "Spurs Complete Sweep to Capture Fourth NBA Title," NBA.com. June 15, 2007. http://www.nba.com/games/20070614/SASCLE/recap.html

page 12 "Tim never had much . . ." Quoted in Chip Brown, "Tim Duncan goes from island life to life in the NBA," TexNews.com. October 26, 1997. http://www.texnews.com/texsports97/duncan102697.html

page 15 "I enjoyed college . . ." Quoted in Josh Staph, "Interview with Tim Duncan," *Stack* Magazine, January 2007. http://magazine.stack.com/TheIssue/ArticleDraw/4081

page 18 "Robinson, a post-up center . . ." Quoted in Jack McCallum, "Sportsmen of the Year: Tim Duncan and David Robinson," SI.com, December 15, 2003. http://robots.cnnsi.com/pr/subs/siexclusive/2003/12/09/sportsmen1215/index.html

page 18 "She knew all about . . ." Quoted in S.L. Price, "The Quiet Man," SI.com, December 15, 2003. http://robots.cnnsi.com/pr/subs/siexclusive/2003/12/08/duncan1215/index.html

page 20 "It's an incredible honor . . ." Quoted in Associated Press, "Duncan: A quiet, boring, dominant MVP," SI.com, June 28, 1999. http://sportsillustrated.cnn.com/basketball/nba/1999/playoffs/news/1999/06/25/duncan_boring/

page 22 "We're all very fortunate . . ." "San Antonio's Tim Duncan Keeps Promise," *Jet* (August 21, 2000), 47.

page 24 "To date, the Tim . . ." Tim Duncan, "The Tim Duncan Foundation." http://www.slamduncan.com/about-foundation.php

page 25 "When I was a kid . . ." Tim Duncan. "21 Questions with Tim Duncan," SlamDuncan.com, printed March 26, 2008. http://www.slamduncan.com/news-21questions.php

page 28 "Duncan was better than ever . . ." Sam Smith, "Why all the fuss? Tim Duncan deserving of MVP," *Chicago Tribune*, May 9, 2002. http://www.accessmylibrary.com/coms2/summary_0286-6817527_ITM

page 29 "It's fun to play . . ." Sean Stewart, "One on One," *The Sporting News* (January 1, 2001), 46.

page 29 "Seattle repeatedly sent . . ." Sean Deveney, "A little bit louder: Tim Duncan still exudes quiet confidence, but he's learning to speak up more as the Spurs try to erase the memory of last season's playoffs," *The Sporting News*, May 6, 2002. http://www.accessmylibrary.com/coms2/summary_0286-26961776_ITM

page 31 "A new Duncan has emerged . . ." Deveney, "A little bit louder: Tim Duncan still exudes quiet confidence, but he's learning to speak up more as the Spurs try to erase the memory of last season's playoffs."

page 35 "Dave's been an incredible part . . ." Tim Duncan, "2003 NBA Finals Postgame Quotes: Game 6," NBA.com, June 15, 2003. http://www.nba.com/spurs/news/quotes_spurs_030615.html#tduncan

page 37 "Duncan plays a stern . . ." Deveney, "A little bit louder: Tim Duncan still exudes quiet confidence, but he's learning to speak up more as the Spurs try to erase the memory of last season's playoffs."

page 41 "In the third quarter . . ." George Gervin, from John Hareas, *One Team. One Goal. Mission Accomplished: The 2005 NBA Champion San Antonio Spurs* (Daytona Beach, FL: EventDay Media, 2005), 108.

page 43 "His basketball legacy . . ." John Hareas, *One Team. One Goal. Mission Accomplished: The 2005 NBA Champion San Antonio Spurs* (Daytona Beach, FL: EventDay Media, 2005), 17.

page 45 "Just got to gear . . ." Associated Press, "Bryant lifts Lakers into NBA Finals as L.A. rallies from 17-point hole," ESPN.com (May 29, 2008). http://scores.espn.go.com/nba/recap?gameId=280529013

page 47 "No question he's the greatest . . ." Quoted in David DuPree, "Tim Duncan: best power forward ever?" USAToday.com, June 6, 2007. http://www.usatoday.com/sports/basketball/nba/spurs/2007-06-06-bonus-duncan_N.htm

page 53 "By acclamation, Michael Jordan . . ." *NBA Encyclopedia.* http://www.nba.com/history/players/jordan_summary.html

Chuck Bednar is an author and freelance writer from Ohio. He has written five additional books, including one on the San Antonio Spurs, as well as more than 1,300 published nonfiction articles. He is currently working as a forum administrator for GoTeamsGo.com.

PICTURE CREDITS

page

1: Nathaniel S. Butler/NBAE/Getty Images
4: Fort Worth Star-Telegram/MCT
7: Akron Beacon Journal/MCT
8: Jesse D. Garrabrant/NBAE/Getty Images
10: KRT Photos
13: Newsday/NMI
14: UPI Photo Archive
16: Charlotte Observer/KRT
19: Orlando Sentinel/KRT
21: Sports Illustrated/NMI
22: NBAE/SPCS
24: SlamDuncan.com/KRT
26: George Bridges/KRT
29: NBAE/SPCS
30: AFP Photos

33: NBAE/Getty Images
34: Chuck Kennedy/KRT
36: Adidas/NMI
39: D. Clarke Evans/NBAE/Getty Images
40: NBAE/SPCS
42: NBAE/SPCS
44: Jesse D. Garrabrant/NBAE/Getty Images
45: D. Clarke Evans/NBAE/Getty Images
46: T&T/IOA Photos
48: T&T/IOS Photos
49: SportsChrome Pix
51: JHMM13/NMI
52: Nathaniel S. Butler/NBAE/Getty Images
53: SportsChrome Pix
55: NBAE/SPCS

Front cover: Nathaniel S. Butler/NBAE/Getty Images

KENILWORTH PUBLIC LIBRARY
548 BOULEVARD
KENILWORTH, N.J. 07033